Greatest
MOMENTS OF
FOOTBALL

This edition first published in the UK in 2007
By Green Umbrella Publishing

© Green Umbrella Publishing 2007

www.greenumbrella.co.uk

Publishers: Jules Gammond and Vanessa Gardner

Printed and bound in China

ISBN: 978-1-906229-39-9

The views in this book are those of the author but they are general views only and readers are urged to consult the relevant and qualified specialist
for individual advice in particular situations.

All our best endeavours have been made to secure copyright clearance for every photograph used but in the event of any copyright owner being overlooked
please address correspondence to Green Umbrella Publishing, The Old Bakehouse, 21 The Street, Lydiard Millicent, Swindon SN5 3LU

Greatest
MOMENTS OF
FOOTBALL

by GRAHAM BETTS

CONTENTS

CONTENTS

BLACKPOOL v
BOLTON WANDERERS 4-3

FA Cup Final – Wembley 2/5/1953

Blackpool:
Farm, Shimwell, Garrett, Fenton, Johnston, Robinson, Matthews, Taylor, Mortensen, Mudie, Perry

Bolton Wanderers:
Hanson, Ball, Banks, Wheeler, Barrass, Bell, Holden, Moir, Lofthouse, Hassall, Langton

Whilst there were many in the Blackpool side who could claim to be almost household names, none had the allure or reputation of Stanley Matthews. A full England international since 1934, his switch from Stoke City to Blackpool for a paltry £11,500 in 1947 had prompted protests from the bemused Stoke fans, aghast that their most prized asset should be allowed to leave so cheaply.

Matthews would form an exceptional understanding with centre-forward Stan Mortensen, one that would propel Mortensen into the national side, and Blackpool were hopeful that the combination would similarly lift them into contention for honours. A place in the 1948 FA Cup final followed, but Manchester United proved resilient enough to come from behind twice to finally win 4-2. Three years later Newcastle United were too strong for them, condemning them to a 2-0 defeat. Rather than contend for major honours, Blackpool seemed destined to be forever collecting runner's-up medals.

Blackpool's appearance in the 1953 final, therefore, was seen by many as a last chance for Stan Matthews to pick up a winner's medal, with much of the country willing him to succeed after two previous disappointments. The exception, of course, were the residents of Bolton, who would be backing Nat Lofthouse, the Lion of Vienna, to get the goals that would return the FA Cup to the town for the first time since 1929. The smart money, however, was on Blackpool, conquerors of the previous year's finalists and soon to be League champions, Arsenal, proof that Blackpool could live with and beat more illustrious opponents.

Blackpool's preparations were hardly helped by injuries to their two Stanleys. Mortensen had struggled with a cartilage problem and had missed two months of the season at the turn of the year and was still straining to achieve full match fitness. Of greater concern was Matthews, who turned up on the morning of the match with a thigh strain, one that was considered bad enough to put his place in the line-up in doubt. News of Matthews' strain was kept within the Blackpool camp and a painkilling injection was administered that would enable him to join seven of his 1951 team-mates in the side for the 1953 final.

Bolton settled the quicker, aided by an opening goal from Nat Lofthouse after just two minutes, with his underhit shot from outside the penalty area bobbling over the shoulder of George Farm and trickling into the net. The goal served to further galvanise Bolton, who launched wave after wave of attacks on Blackpool without adding to their tally. Then on 18 minutes Bolton's Eric Bell pulled a hamstring, leaving him little more than a passenger for the rest of the game. His switch to a less demanding role on the left wing meant he had a presence, but his injury would eventually prove an important factor. Despite Bell's handicap Bolton continued to press forward, with Lofthouse hitting the post after some 20 minutes. At last Blackpool awoke from their slumbers, with Stan Mortensen grabbing an equaliser with a cross-shot that took a deflection off Hassall before crossing the line on 35 minutes. Parity was restored for just five minutes, with Moir being

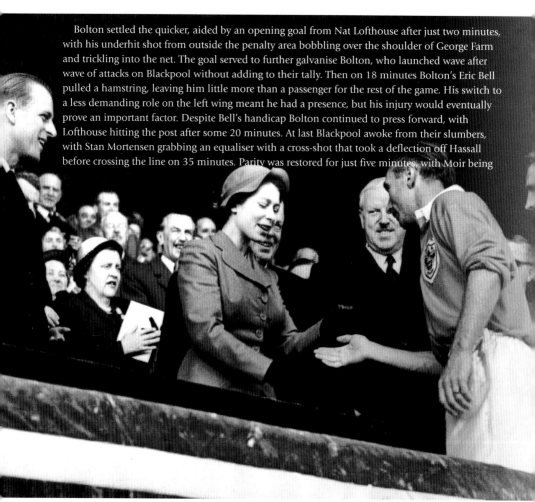

credited with Bolton's second when he lunged at a speculative cross from Langton, although later replays suggested he had not got a touch to the ball. Whoever got the credit, the blame rested with George Farm for failing to deal with a cross he would normally gather up with ease.

The second half saw little let up in Bolton's attack and 10 minutes after the break the still limping Eric Bell seemed to have made the match safe with a header that put Bolton 3-1 ahead. There was surely no way back now for Blackpool.

Stan Matthews had been a shadow of his former self for the first hour of the match, but Bolton's problems on the left began to work in his favour. As well as the limping Eric Bell, left-back Ralph Banks was hindered by shin cramps, and Blackpool at last realised that the right wing, Stan's wing, might provide the route back into the game. Ernie Taylor began supplying the ball to Matthews on a regular basis and Stan began turning the defenders this way and that in search of the byline. On 68 minutes he found the line and pulled the ball back towards the goal. Stan Hanson in the Bolton goal was only able to touch it into the path of the onrushing Mortensen to make the score 3-2 and give Blackpool belief that they might rescue the game.

Bolton weathered the next 20 minutes, their defensive efforts ever more frantic as Blackpool pressed for an equaliser. With just two minutes left on the clock Blackpool were awarded a free-kick on the edge of the penalty area, with Mortensen lining up to take a shot. A Bolton defender pulled away to mark the approaching Shimwell and in an instant Mortensen had spotted the gap and buried the ball into the net for the equaliser and completed his own hat-trick.

Everyone seemed to accept extra time as inevitable, everyone except Stan Matthews. The game was deep into injury time and referee Griffiths had already checked his watch as Stan Matthews made his way down the right wing for one last time. Looking up he saw that Mortensen was heavily marked, but Bill Perry appeared to have room to spare, so Matthews played the ball through to the South African, slipping as he did so. Perry hit the ball goalwards first time with his right foot and saw it evade the desperate lunges of two Bolton defenders before nestling in the corner of the net. From two goals down, Blackpool had finally got ahead 4-3, with barely time to restart the match.

Nat Lofthouse was gracious enough to applaud the winning goal and Blackpool's players showed who had been responsible for their victory; after being presented with the trophy, they chaired captain Harry Johnston as was traditional and Stanley Matthews around the pitch. Even now, more than 50 years later, the match is recalled as the Matthews Final, the contributions of Mortensen and Lofthouse and 19 others completely overshadowed by one man.

REAL MADRID v EINTRACHT FRANKFURT 7-3

European Cup Final – Hampden Park 18/5/1960

Real Madrid:
Dominguez, Marquitos, Santamaria, Pachin, Vidal, Zarraga, Canario, Del Sol, Di Stefano, Puskas, Gento

Eintracht Frankfurt:
Loy, Lutz, Eigenbrodt, Hofer, Weilbacher, Stinka, Kress, Lindner, Stein, Pfaff, Meier

Ask any football fan to name the greatest game ever played and he will inevitably select one that features his own team, an expected and fairly normal reaction. But ask one of the 135,000 plus in attendance or those who have seen the match on television, whether 'live' or on video, and many will plump for the 1960 European Cup final between Real Madrid and Eintracht Frankfurt at Hampden Park.

The appeal of the match was obvious – Real Madrid were the dominant force in European club football, having won all of the previous four European Cup competitions. Their side had been further strengthened by the acquisition, albeit through complex and at times bizarre circumstances, of Ferenc Puskas, the former Galloping Major who had taken the opportunity of defecting from Hungary whilst the 1956 revolution was in full swing. After being forced out of the game through the lack of a player registration form, he had turned up at Real Madrid where it was initially believed he was too old and too fat to be of much use. A strict training regime trimmed him down to size and, whilst he could do little to halt the advancing years, he showed enough guile in practice to convince the club that his mind was as sharp as ever – he still had much to offer. Puskas had helped Real Madrid reach the final in 1959 but was omitted from the line-up as he was not fully fit – Real Madrid were not going to make the same mistake the Hungarian national coach had in 1954 and select a player only half fit.

Many in the crowd at Hampden were convinced that there existed a team capable of ending Real Madrid's domination and that that side was Eintracht Frankfurt. Their confidence was based on the

comprehensive way Eintracht had seen off Rangers in the semi-final, winning 6-1 in Frankfurt and 6-3 in Glasgow for a 12-4 aggregate win. They also had a certain degree of experience in their side, not least Alfred Pfaff, a member of the West German side that had beaten Hungary in 1954, and the supposed added advantage of being all German, as compared with the multi-national composition of their opponents (Real Madrid had taken advantage of the rules in force at the time

to make Di Stefano and Santamaria Spanish citizens and had filled the overseas players slots with Didi and Canario from Brazil).

Puskas had no doubt as to the outcome of the match, stating before kick-off, "Every man in our team is an attacker and we have the quality so many British sides envy. That is to be able to pull something out of the bag when things are not going well. Many people thought we were tired and would not win our semi-final against Barcelona but my quick goal gave us an advantage. Indeed it is our policy to go for an early lead in every game." There was to be an early goal in the final, but it was scored by Eintracht, Kress volleying in a low cross after three earlier attempts had severely rattled Real Madrid.

Going a goal down served to wake Real from their slumbers and almost immediately Gento hit the outside of the post by way of a response. A few moments later Di Stefano was put through by Canario and levelled the scores, also maintaining his record of having scored in every European Cup final. Real kept up the momentum and took the lead two minutes later, Di Stefano reacting quickest after Loy had fumbled a Canario shot.

Alfredo Di Stefano was now effectively running the match, at the heart of all of Real's moves and orchestrating the game, spraying out passes to Gento, Canario and Puskas as Real ran the Germans ragged. Just before half-time Puskas extended Real's lead to 3-1, firing into the roof of the net from an extremely tight angle, and 10 minutes after the break scored from the penalty spot following a foul by Lutz. Puskas, in his first European Cup final, added a further two goals, a header from close range and a shot from 18 yards to give Real a 6-1 lead and effective victory with 20 minutes to play.

Having been given the run around for 70 or so minutes Eintracht managed to drag themselves back into the game with a goal from Stein, but that served only to inspire Di Stefano to even greater heights; collecting the ball inside the centre circle, he brushed away one opponent, played a one-two with a colleague that took two Germans out of the game and, darting into the penalty area shot powerfully into the goal to claim a hat-trick. Even that was not the end of the scoring, Stein grabbing a late consolation for an Eintracht side that battled gamely until the final whistle. It was the Germans' lot to have scored first and last but they had been swept aside by some of the most breathtaking and exhilarating football ever witnessed. The crowd obviously thought so, giving Real a 45-minute ovation that lasted long after the trophy had been presented to captain Zarraga. The longest cheers were reserved for Puskas, who scored four goals and Di Stefano, who got the other three. For once the master had been eclipsed, but Real Madrid had won their fifth straight European Cup, more than adequate compensation.

BENFICA v
REAL MADRID 3-2

European Cup Final – Amsterdam 2/5/1962

Benfica:
Costa Pereira, Mario Joao, Germano, Angelo, Caven, Cruz, Jose Augusto, Eusebio, Aguas, Colluna, Simoes

Real Madrid:
Araquistain, Casado, Santamaria, Miera, Felo, Pachin, Tejada, Del Sol, Di Stefano, Puskas, Gento

Real Madrid's European Cup final clash with Eintracht Frankfurt in 1960 had been acknowledged perhaps the best game ever played, but this was almost entirely because of the performance of Real, with their opponents cast in little more than a supporting role. The 1962 final, which pitted Real against Benfica, has similarly entered folklore, but this time around because both sides contributed towards a memorable final.

Real's reign as European champions had come to an end in the second round of the 1960-61 competition, but it was not their victors, fellow Spanish side Barcelona who assumed the mantle of champions but another side from the Iberian Peninsular, Benfica. Built around such players as Mario Coluna, Jose Augusto and, perhaps most famously of all Eusebio, Benfica had overwhelmed Barcelona in the final after coming from behind.

Real and Benfica made their way to the 1962 final with conflicting performances at the semi-final stage, Real easy victors over Standard Liege and Benfica surviving an onslaught against Tottenham Hotspur. The final, therefore, pitted the only two sides to have won the European Cup, a fitting finale for the 1961-62 season.

Real may have been an ageing side, still reliant on the likes of Puskas, Di Stefano and Gento, but with age came experience, and no club possessed it quite like Real Madrid. Benfica began the match looking as though their only intention was to give Real the run around and wait for tiredness to set in, but there was too much ability and experience within the Real side to fall for

that particular game. Instead, Real allowed Benfica to stretch themselves, then caught them with a classic counter attack after only 17 minutes, Puskas collecting the ball on the halfway line and firing home the opener. Six minutes later Puskas extended the lead, shooting from the edge of the penalty area, with the ball swerving and then bouncing away from the deceived goalkeeper and into the net.

With just over 20 minutes gone Benfica appeared dead and buried, but they were quick to find a route back, Aguas reacting quickest after a Eusebio shot had hit the post. Nine minutes later they pulled level, Cavern firing in a shot from 25 yards that Araquistain later claimed he 'lost' in the inadequate floodlighting. Four minutes later, however, Puskas completed his hat-trick to restore Real's lead, a lead they held going into the half-time break.

The 10-minute break turned out to eventually be more vital than the 90 minutes' football. With Real Madrid ahead, there was no need to change the tactics that had worked so spectacularly over the previous seven years – the formation would remain the same, confident that the outcome would remain the same. In the Benfica dressing room, however, Hungarian coach Bela Guttmann worked his magic, instructing Cavern to man mark Di Stefano, the man who created the chances for the likes of Puskas to despatch. With the supply line cut, he reasoned, Real would not be such a force, leaving his own formidable strikers such as Eusebio free to plunder at will.

Guttmann's instincts proved correct. Alfredo Di Stefano hardly got a touch during the second period, shadowed throughout by Cavern, and with Di Stefano rendered ineffective, so Puskas and Gento similarly disappeared from view. Benfica exploited the gaps and Coluna pulled them level a second time on the hour mark with another long range shot that left Araquistain a helpless bystander. An injury to defender Pedro Casado left him a virtual passenger out on the wing, a further blow to Real Madrid.

Then Eusebio entered the fray, using his youth and his pace to outstrip Di Stefano before being pulled down in the area for a penalty. Eusebio picked himself up to fire home the kick himself and put Benfica ahead for the first time in the match. Ten minutes later he worked a short kick routine with Coluna to fire home Benfica's fifth goal and finally put a bit of space between them and their opponents. There was still time for Real to have their own penalty claim, the referee being unconvinced after Di Stefano had been brought down in the area (he was probably the only man in the stadium who didn't think it was a penalty) and a later shot from the same player that hit the goalkeeper on the legs whilst he was floundering in another direction.

The final whistle brought mixed emotions – Eusebio ran almost 30 yards to offer his red shirt as a swap with the blue one belonging to Puskas (quite why Real wore blue has never been adequately explained, since blue and red would have been something of a clash to those watching on black and white television sets!), as symbolic a gesture of the old handing over to the new as there has ever been. The other Real great, Alfredo Di Stefano, meanwhile, took the defeat badly, not bothering to collect his runner's-up medal and storming off the field for the sanctity of the dressing room, followed by most of his sheepish team-mates. Benfica collected the cup for the second consecutive and, though they weren't to know it, the last time.

ENGLAND v
WEST GERMANY 4-2

World Cup Final – Wembley 30/7/1966

England:
Banks, Cohen, Wilson, Stiles, J Charlton, Moore, Ball, Hurst, R Charlton, Hunt, Peters

West Germany:
Tilkowski, Höttges, Weber, Schulz, Schnellinger, Beckenbauer, Haller, Overath, Seeler, Held, Emmerich

Upon his appointment as England manager in October 1963, Alf Ramsey told the assembled press that his side would win the 1966 World Cup. It appeared at the time to be the height of folly, for England had struggled to impress in any of the previous tournaments they had competed in, going no further than the quarter-finals in 1954 and 1962. But Ramsey had reason for confidence, not least of which was that as hosts, England would be spared the inconvenience of having to qualify, giving them extra time to prepare.

Over the next three years Alf Ramsey fashioned a side capable of competing at the highest level. In contrast to the almost schoolteacher manner of his predecessor Walter Winterbottom, Alf Ramsey wanted his players to treat him as one of the lads, even to the extent of calling him Alf. In this way he could foster a club spirit within an international squad, something of a rarity.

England's first game in pursuit of the ultimate prize saw them struggle to break down a resolute Uruguayan defence, leading many of those watching to believe England would fare no better in 1966 than they had in 1962. Eventual victories over France and Mexico saw England qualify out of their group as winners, but thereafter Ramsey began ringing the changes. It was always claimed that as a former full-back he naturally hated wingers, but this was not the case. During his playing days he had performed with and against the likes of Stanley Matthews and Tom Finney, and he had used wingers during the early World Cup matches. But the players he had were not of the quality of their predecessors, and Ramsey needed a bit more guile to make further progress in the competition.

The so called wingless wonders played with a 4-4-2 formation, making England extremely difficult to break down. With the likes of Alan Ball prepared to run all day, England were a hardworking side. And in Geoff Hurst, they had a goalscorer of proven ability and good with both his head and feet. This new look England made it into the final, where they would face West Germany.

The West Germans had identified Bobby Charlton as England's key player and detailed the young Franz Beckenbauer to mark him out of the game. Beckenbauer stuck to his task and did a remarkable job, but unfortunately he also blunted his own worth to the German side, for he had scored a number of crucial goals in the German run to the final.

As it was, the first goal came as a result of a mistake, Ray Wilson's first (and only) one of the competition when he weakly headed out a cross straight to the feet of Helmut Haller who shot home first time. England were level five minutes later, Geoff Hurst rising to head home a Bobby Moore free-kick whilst the Germans were still organising their defence. It was another set piece that enabled England to take the lead a further 12 minutes on, Alan Ball's corner leading to a Hurst shot that was blocked and looped upwards, arching invitingly for Martin Peters to volley home what appeared to be a decisive winner.

With time running out the Germans became more desperate in their attempts to draw level. Jackie Charlton was ajudged to have committed a foul just outside the England penalty area and was still protesting his innocence when Emmerich sent in a cross. The ball whistled across the England goal, seemingly helped on by the hand of Schnellinger before falling at the feet of Weber at the far post to prod home the equaliser.

England were crestfallen at being pegged back so late in the game, but Ramsey quickly moved among his players during the break before extra time to lift their spirits. Firstly he told them to remain standing so that their opponents would believe they were still full of running. Then he told them they'd won the competition once, now they had to go out and do it again.

The resulting 30 minutes of extra time has entered folklore. England created most, if not all of the chances and took two of them, but the first 'goal' is still hotly debated and disputed. Geoff Hurst received the ball inside the German penalty area and in a single movement, spun and fired in a shot with his right foot. The ball hit the underside of the bar and dropped down onto the line, bouncing up again high enough for a German defender to head it over the bar. England's players called for a goal, but the referee was unsure whether it had crossed the line so went to consult with the linesman. Although Tofik Bakhramov was at least 50 yards from the incident and not even up with play (he was 10 yards off the goalline) he signalled a goal and England were 3-2 ahead. In the final moments, Bobby Moore put Hurst through with just a defender for company and the goalkeeper to beat and fired home the first and still only hat-trick in a World Cup final to secure a 4-2 England victory.

England captain Bobby Moore thoughtfully wiped his hand as he made his way up towards the Royal Box at Wembley, extended it to shake the hand of the Queen and then received the Jules Rimet Trophy, the only major trophy England have ever won. Just as Alf Ramsey said they would.

CELTIC v
INTER MILAN 2-1

European Cup Final – Lisbon, 25/5/1967

Celtic:
Simpson, Craig, McNeill, Clark, Gemmell, Murdoch, Auld, Johnstone, Wallace, Chalmers, Lennox

Inter Milan:
Sarti, Burgnich, Guameri, Picchi, Facchetti, Bedin, Mazzola, Bicicli, Domenghini, Cappellini, Corso

Jock Stein enjoyed a distinguished career as a Celtic player, helping them win the domestic double of League and Scottish FA Cup in 1954 before being forced to retire owing to a series of niggling injuries two years later. After a spell in charge of Celtic's youth and reserve teams, Jock looked to pursue a career as a manager, moving on to Dunfermline and then Hibernian and enjoying success of sorts at both clubs.

By the time he answered the call to return to Celtic Park in 1965 his former club had not tasted success in either the League or FA Cup since that double dose in 1954. They had not won any major competition since the League Cup in 1958 and had been surpassed not only by bitter rivals Rangers but also Hearts, Dundee and Kilmarnock in the domestic game. Jock Stein turned the club around and in 1966 they won the League and League Cup and reached the semi-finals of the European Cup Winners' Cup. This latter competition would provide them with considerable experience of performing in Europe for the following season's European Cup, their first such tilt at the premier club competition.

Jock Stein's attention to detail, careful planning and tactical awareness enabled them to negotiate their way past FC Zurich, Nantes, Vojvodina and Dukla Prague to make the final in Lisbon, where they would face the ultra-defensive Italian side Inter Milan.

Inter's coach, Helenio Herrera was almost the match of Jock Stein. He too left nothing to chance in the preparation of his side for the final, including getting his reserve side to line up in formation

in what he believed to be Celtic's style, even down to having the reserves wear their numbers on their shorts (a fashion unique to Celtic until ordered to put them on the backs of their shirts by UEFA many years later). But some things he could not prepare for, not least losing his Brazilian winger Jair to a knee injury and Spanish midfielder Luis Suarez with a thigh strain. By comparison to the cosmopolitan line-up employed by Inter, all of Celtic's players were born pretty much within a goal-kick of Celtic Park.

GREATEST MOMENTS OF FOOTBALL

As the Estadio Nacional had no floodlights, the match kicked off in the middle of the afternoon, making it especially hot for the 22 players. The temperature rose considerably after only six minutes when Jim Craig, under pressure, committed a foul on Renato Cappellini and brought him down inside the penalty area, although Celtic protested strongly at the giving of a penalty. Sandro Mazzola, whose original ball into the area had brought about the award, stepped up to take the penalty and duly sent it into the left-hand corner of the net for the opening goal.

Despite the feeling of injustice at the time (later replays showed it was a penalty), Celtic didn't let the decision play on their minds. Instead they took the game to Inter and made goalkeeper Giuliano Sarti the busier of the two custodians for the remainder of the match. They were also helped by Inter's natural instinct to defend the lead they had achieved, even if there was still more than 80 minutes left to play – the Italian side were past masters at achieving victory with a 1-0 scoreline.

Although they had much the larger percentage of the play and having hit the bar, Celtic arrived at half-time still trailing. Jock Stein had little to say to his side other than keep playing the way they were and the rewards would come, but if anything, Celtic stepped up their efforts in the second half, especially the midfield prompting of Bobby Murdoch and Bertie Auld. Finally, with just over an hour played, Celtic drew level, full-back Tommy Gemmell doing what he did at domestic level and overlapping down the wing to thrash home a cross from Jim Craig from 25 yards. All of the Celtic players knew then that there was only going to be one winner, as Stevie Chalmers later pointed out. 'Their heads went down. We knew then we were going to win it.'

Having defended for more than an hour, Inter did not have the ability to come out of their shell and re-impose themselves on the game, so Celtic kept up the pressure. With just eight minutes left on the clock the winning goal came, a Bobby Murdoch cross was deflected by Chalmers past Sarti and Celtic were on their way, crowned champions of Europe at the first time of asking. In the dressing room after the game, Liverpool manager and fellow Scot Bill Shankly told the Celtic manager 'John, you're immortal.'

Whilst the success made heroes out of the 11 players and one manager, the Celtic fans had also played their part and the stories of their experiences were equally legendary. Some never made it home, preferring to remain in Portugal where they live and work to this day. Many others arrived home days after the final, still hung over, and alighted the countless coaches and planes that ferried the fans around Europe, only to remember too late they had driven out to the final! It was that kind of match, that kind of memory.

ENGLAND v
SCOTLAND 2-3

Home International – Wembley 15/4/1967

England:
Banks, Cohen, Wilson, Stiles, J Charlton, Moore, Ball, Greaves, R Charlton, Hurst, Peters

Scotland:
Simpson, Gemmell, McCreadie, Greig, McKinnon, Bremner, McCalliog, Law, Wallace, Baxter, Lennox

England met Scotland in the very first international match in 1872 and had clashed almost annually thereafter. Whilst there were numerous clubs, particularly south of the border, that had English and Scottish players within the same club line-ups, the rivalry at international level was the most intense in the world. Not for nothing were they described as the best of enemies.

England had won the World Cup in 1966 and no doubt there was much banter between the England players and their Scottish colleagues at club level throughout the following season. Although the media might like to have portrayed an image of England's win as being a success for the whole of Britain, the reality was entirely different.

Manchester United, for example, had provided Bobby Charlton and Nobby Stiles to the victorious England side, and yet team-mate Denis Law, of Scotland, chose not to watch the final, preferring to spend the time on a golf course. He later described the moment when he walked in to the club house and discovered that England were world champions as the worst moment of his life!

The Home International championship match between the foes had an extra ingredient too, for it had been decided that the competition for the 1966-67 and 1967-68 seasons would constitute a qualifying group for the European Championships, with the ultimate winners going into the quarter-finals. Thus when Scotland arrived at Wembley, they needed to win to lift the Home International championship and top the European qualifying group for the first time.

England's side showed only one change from the successful World Cup winning side, Jimmy Greaves instead of Roger Hunt. There was still no place for a recognised winger, Alf Ramsey preferring to dominate and win the match in midfield rather than on the flanks. In this he was helped in having such a willing runner as Alan Ball, as he had proved during the World Cup campaign.

Scotland gave a first cap to Ronnie Simpson, the 36-year-old goalkeeper of the recently successful European champions Celtic, whilst Jim McCalliog, then of Sheffield Wednesday, also came in for an international debut. The Scottish side therefore comprised six players from north of the border and five who plied their trade in England.

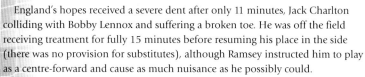

England's hopes received a severe dent after only 11 minutes, Jack Charlton colliding with Bobby Lennox and suffering a broken toe. He was off the field receiving treatment for fully 15 minutes before resuming his place in the side (there was no provision for substitutes), although Ramsey instructed him to play as a centre-forward and cause as much nuisance as he possibly could.

Jack Charlton had barely returned to the field when Scotland took the lead. Willie Wallace shot goalward, but Gordon Banks appeared to have the shot covered when Denis Law diverted it away from Banks' hands. Although Banks re-adjusted himself enough to stop the ball with his feet, Law pounced on the rebound to strike home.

Despite a concerted England attempt to get back on level terms, Scotland held firm to and beyond half-time. As the game entered the final 15 minutes, England's efforts became ever more desperate, leaving gaps at the back that Scotland could exploit. With 78 minutes on the clock, Scotland extended their lead, Law turning provider to lay the ball into the path of the onrushing Bobby Lennox to smash home for a second Scottish goal.

Jack Charlton played through the pain barrier (one of three England players suffering some sort of injury during the course of the match) and got some tangible reward for his efforts, beating two defenders on the line to a pass from Alan Ball to reduce the deficit with some six minutes left to play. Unfortunately the two-goal lead was restored three minutes later, debutant Jim McCalliog playing a one-two with Willie Wallace before firing home a shot that beat the normally excellently-placed Gordon Banks at the near post. There was still time for one more goal, Geoff Hurst heading home Jack Charlton's cross, but it was scant consolation.

The Scottish reacted as though they had won the World Cup, rather than becoming the first side to beat England since that fateful day the previous July. Hordes of Scottish supporters flocked onto the pitch and dug up clumps of turf to take home as souvenirs, whilst the media reaction in certain sections (at least north of the border) proclaimed Scotland as the new world champions! The euphoria didn't last long, for England won the following year's Home International championship and grabbed the qualifying place for the European Championships.

MANCHESTER UNITED v BENFICA 4-1

European Cup Final – Wembley, 29/5/1968

Manchester United:
Stepney, Brennan, Foulkes, Crerand, Dunne, Charlton, Stiles, Best, Kidd, Sadler, Aston

Benfica:
Henrique, Adolfo, Humberto, Jacinto, Cruz, Graca, Coluna, Jose Augusto, Torres, Eusebio, Simoes

Ever since they had first earned the right to compete in the European Champions Clubs' Cup (or European Cup, as it became more commonly known) in 1956, Manchester United and their manager Matt Busby had viewed the competition as something of a holy grail. They had reached the semi-final in 1957 before being beaten by the holders Real Madrid, but the only thing Busby claimed his side lacked was experience – they would be a better side the following year. Busby and Manchester United never got a chance to find out how good they could have become, for after qualifying for the semi-final again, the plane carrying them back from Belgrade crashed in Munich and the bulk of their side lost their lives. A patched up United side was no match for Milan over two legs and they exited the competition at the penultimate stage once again.

It was to take Matt Busby eight years before he got another tilt at the European Cup, reaching the semi-finals for a third time and once again falling, this time to Partizan Belgrade. Two years later, in the year that would see the poignant tenth anniversary of the Munich disaster, United qualified again. This time they made it through to the final, seeing off Real Madrid in the semi-final after a great fightback in the second leg in Madrid. Their opponents were to be Benfica, a side they had beaten on their run in 1966 but who were appearing in their fifth final in just eight years.

The final threw up a number of interesting confrontations, not least of which was the battle between United's Nobby Stiles and Benfica's Eusebio, who had memorably been in opposition in the World Cup semi-final for England and Portugal respectively in 1966. Then Stiles had put in a

BENFICA 0   MANCHESTER U. 0

masterful man-marking job, keeping Eusebio quiet for most of the 90 minutes, without once having to resort to anything untoward with regards his tackling. Two years on Stiles would repeat the performance, leaving the Black Pearl almost lacklustre.

United's desire proved stronger in the opening exchanges, but the first half was still a tense affair with neither side able to make any noticeable headway. Then, seven minutes into the second half,

United at last made a breakthrough, David Sadler crossing in from the wing and Bobby Charlton, a survivor from Munich, getting the merest of touches with his head to direct the ball past Henrique. Forced to chase the game Benfica came back strongly and created a number of chances, but as the game entered the final 10 minutes United looked capable of holding on. Then Torres beat Foulkes to a header and played the ball downwards, with Jaime Graca arriving in time to shoot home past Stepney. United's heads dropped momentarily, seemingly pegged back just as they were on the verge of achieving the win. Worse could and should have hit them five minutes later, for Eusebio lost Stiles for about the only time during the match and bore down on goal with only Stepney to beat. With virtually the whole goal to aim for, Eusebio chose to shoot straight and the chance was lost. Eusebio was gentlemanly enough to shake a surprised Stepney's hand immediately after the incident, perhaps implying that the keeper had made a good save, but it did not disguise a wayward miss, one which Eusebio and Benfica would come to rue.

The game was to go into extra time, with Matt Busby hurrying onto the Wembley pitch to deliver a fresh set of instructions to his deflated troops. Whatever he said worked wonders, for having been so close to defeat, United played the additional half an hour like men possessed. Barely two minutes into extra time United restored their lead, a long punt from Stepney being headed on by Brian Kidd and collected by the mercurial George Best. The United player Benfica feared above all others had had a quiet match, by his standards, but lit up the game in an instant. He beat Cruz with ease and headed towards goal, drawing out Henrique from the goal and, with a simple dummy, took the keeper out and created a gaping hole in which to shoot. It was an audacious yet magical goal, the kind only George Best could score.

Benfica's attempts to get level the first time had drained their capabilities and as extra time progressed, United looked more like adding to their tally. A Charlton corner was headed on at the near post by David Sadler to Brian Kidd, on his nineteenth birthday, who headed goalwards. Henrique saved his first attempt but Kidd nodded the rebound beyond his reach. Two minutes from time came the final goal, a Kidd cross being met by a second Bobby Charlton header that looped up and over the despairing goalkeeper.

The final whistle was met with pandemonium as Matt Busby raced onto the pitch to hail his heroes, reserving his longest and most heartfelt hugs for Bobby Charlton and Bill Foulkes, who had survived Munich with him. Even Benfica did not begrudge Busby, Charlton, Foulkes and the younger United players their moment of glory, the culmination of a dream that had risen from the ashes and snow of Munich 10 years previously.

WEST GERMANY v ENGLAND 3-2

World Cup Quarter-final – Leon 14/6/1970

West Germany:
Maier, Vogts, Fichtel, Schnellinger, Hottges (Schulz), Seeler, Beckenbauer, Overath, Libuda (Grabowski), Muller, Lohr

England:
Bonetti, Newton, Cooper, Mullery, Labone, Moore, Lee, Ball, Hurst, R Charlton (Bell), Peters (Hunter)

England's World Cup victory in 1966 had been predicted by manager Alf Ramsey. Four years later, in the heat and altitude of Mexico, he confidently expected to retain the trophy, believing he had an even stronger squad this time around. There was still no place for wingers, but there were plenty of combative midfield players to more than make up for their absence.

Most of England's problems originated off the field – Ramsey's public relations disaster a year before the tournament kicked off, when he announced that England would be taking all of their food requirements with them, together with a bus shipped over for the occasion, coupled with the attempt to frame captain Bobby Moore for stealing a gold bracelet when the team were in Colombia to play a warm up match, had attracted all the wrong kind of publicity.

The game in 1970 was different from four years previously too, for with substitutes now permitted and not just for injuries, it had become a 13-man game. Making changes midway through a game to try and change the match or preserve key players was an important part of the managerial role.

England had been unimpressive in their group matches, being cautious in their 1-0 victories over Romania and Czechoslovakia that had enabled them to progress into the quarter-finals. They had been much better, especially goalkeeper Gordon Banks, in the 1-0 defeat by Brazil, leading many, including Alf Ramsey, to believe that the two sides were destined to meet in the final. England would have to negotiate their way past West Germany and, most likely Italy, in order to make the final in their half of the draw.

England's plans against West Germany began to unravel two days before the sides were due to meet. Gordon Banks drank from a bottle of beer and was then taken ill with a stomach upset. It was enough to keep him out of the side, gifting a place to Chelsea's Peter Bonetti, his seventh cap for his country. Both sides lined up with five players who had played in the 1966 final meeting, with Franz Beckenbauer again given the task of marking Bobby Charlton.

It was Alan Mullery, playing in the role previously occupied by Nobby Stiles that gave England a deserved lead from six yards as they at last began to play like world champions. Five minutes into the second half the lead was extended, a hitherto anonymous Martin Peters ghosting in at the far post to slot home a second.

With nothing to lose, German manager Helmut Schoen shook his side up, taking off Libuda to bring on the winger Grabowski and instructing Beckenbauer to leave his defensive duties on Charlton and aid the attack. It worked too, for after 57 minutes, Beckenbauer rounded Mullery and shot unconvincingly from a tight angle and the ball somehow squirmed under the body of a nervous Peter Bonetti.

Ramsey responded with his own tactical changes, taking off Charlton in order to preserve his energies for the expected semi-final and replacing him with Colin Bell. Whilst Bell's contribution would ultimately be minimal, the departure of Charlton allowed Beckenbauer to be ever more adventurous, and it was through him that virtually every German attack thereafter originated. Ramsey then took off Peters to bring on Norman Hunter, effectively spelling the end of England as a creative unit in this match, but his reasoning was that no England side under his control had ever lost a two-goal lead, and this England side were still ahead on the day.

That was to remain the case until nine minutes from time when Uwe Seeler scored with a looping header that caught Bonetti stranded in no-man's land. Although Ramsey came onto the field at the end of normal time to deliver a repeat of his 'you've beaten them once, go and beat them again' speech of four years previously, the England side left on the field at the end of the game in 1970 was not of the same calibre of four years previously. Despite their shortcomings, creativity being the key one, England started extra time fired up and carried the game to the Germans, looking to restore their lead. Geoff Hurst looked to have done just that but found his effort mysteriously disallowed. Then Gerd Muller put West Germany ahead for the first time, volleying home from close in with Bonetti again rooted to the spot.

England threw everything into the attack in the last few moments that remained but could find no way through and slipped out of the World Cup, not to return for a good 12 years. It marked the end of the international career of Bobby Charlton – he would not be needed for the semi-final after all! Most of the blame after the game was directed towards Peter Bonetti, the Chelsea goalkeeper, having a game he and most of England would rather forget, but it should also be remembered that England eventually suffered because of the over-cautious approach of Al Ramsey, one of the few mistakes he made whilst in charge of his country.

ARSENAL v
MANCHESTER UNITED 3-2

FA Cup Final – Wembley 12/5/1979

Arsenal:
Jennings, Rice, Nelson, Talbot, O'Leary, Young, Brady, Sunderland, Stapleton, Price (Walford), Rix

Manchester United:
Bailey, Nicholl, Albiston, McIlroy, McQueen, Buchan, Coppell, Greenhoff, Jordan, Macari, Thomas

Whilst Arsenal and Manchester United were undoubtedly among the most illustrious names of the domestic game, the two sides that met in the FA Cup final in 1979 were two sides in the midst of consolidation and rebuilding. Arsenal's last success in any competition had come at the start of the decade, when they had won the double, whilst Manchester United had suffered the pain of relegation before being restored to the top flight and winning the FA Cup in 1977 against Liverpool, denying the Anfield club the treble that United themselves were to win some 22 years later.

Both clubs had had their ups and downs on the way to Wembley. Arsenal had needed five matches before finally getting past Third Division Sheffield Wednesday in the third round and then a replay in the sixth round against Southampton, making it 10 matches before they got to the twin towers. Manchester United also needed replays in the fourth round (against Fulham), sixth round (against Tottenham) and semi-final (against Liverpool), making it eight games before arriving at Wembley.

United's side for the day contained seven of the players who had won the FA Cup against Liverpool two years previously, although it represented something of a gamble in selecting Jimmy Greenhoff, troubled by a pelvic strain and not at his best during the match. Arsenal, for their part, had nine of the side that had lost the final the previous season against Ipswich Town and had added Brian Talbot from that Ipswich side to their own line-up. Only Pat Rice remained from the triumph in 1971, the last link with the double side.

It was the younger guns that Arsenal had relied upon, in particular the creative talents of Liam Brady and Graham Rix in midfield. If Brady and Rix provided the inspiration, then the leg work was done by Brian Talbot, something of a workhorse who would run and run in pursuit of the ball and then look to lay it off to either of his more talented midfield team-mates.

It was Brady who took control of the game first, collecting the ball inside the centre circle and beating off the challenges of three United players before finding Frank Stapleton wide on the wing.

Stapleton played the ball in to David Price, who side-stepped Buchan and crossed to the edge of the six-yard line, to where Brian Talbot and Alan Sunderland lurked menacingly. Either player could have scored, but it was Talbot who got the vital touch, stabbing home past Bailey for the opener.

Two minutes before the half-time break Arsenal extended their lead, with Liam Brady again at the heart of the move that culminated in the goal. This time he beat just two United players, Albiston and Buchan, but by now he was virtually on the byline, and glancing up long enough to spot Frank Stapleton, sent in an inch-perfect chip onto the Irishman's head. Frank Stapleton seldom missed from six yards and this was no exception – Arsenal went in for the break two goals ahead and with United seemingly lost on how to combat the midfield roaming of Liam Brady and Graham Rix.

United tried to step up the pace in the second half, with Joe Jordan eventually winning more of his battles with Willie Young than he lost, but still the service into the danger areas was minimal, Brady, Rix and Talbot holding the advantage as the second half progressed. After 20 minutes, Arsenal manager Terry Neill took off David Price and put on another defender in Steve Walford, intending to further stifle United's attacking options. Instead the change seemed to benefit United, for it meant less pressure on them further up the field.

Still, with five minutes left to play United had not made any inroads into Arsenal's two-goal advantage. Then a Steve Coppell free-kick on the right found Jordan on the left and his cut back was met by Gordon McQueen to put into the net from seven yards. Despite the goal many felt it was no more than consolation for United, still a goal behind and with just four minutes left on the clock.

Two minutes later United were level, Sammy McIlroy scoring an individual goal of such quality it was good enough to have won the cup. Collecting the ball from Steve Coppell, McIlroy had beaten David O'Leary, nutmegged Steve Walford and placed the ball under the body of Pat Jennings as he dived to bring the scores level. Mentally, United began preparing for extra time, for now there was only two minutes left to play.

Whilst Arsenal were undoubtedly crestfallen, Liam Brady still sensed there was time to put matters right. This time he spotted Graham Rix in space on the left wing and, after a turn of speed had taken him past Macari and Thomas, delivered a pass for Rix to run onto. Rix in turn hit the ball first time in towards goal, with Gary Bailey misjudging the flight and watching it sail over his head. There still seemed little danger, for Arthur Albiston was in place to head the ball away, but the ball fell suddenly before Albiston could apply a touch and Alan Sunderland stretched out a foot to poke the ball into an empty net. This time there was to be no coming back from the dead for United; the cup belonged to Arsenal after the most dramatic five-minute spell the final had ever witnessed

TOTTENHAM HOTSPUR v MANCHESTER CITY 3-2

FA Cup Final – Wembley 14/5/1981

Tottenham Hotspur:
Aleksic, Hughton, Miller, Roberts, Villa, Perryman, Ardiles, Archibald, Galvin, Hoddle, Crooks

Manchester City:
Corrigan, Ranson, McDonald (Tueart), Reid, Gow, Caton, Power, MacKenzie, Reeves, Bennett, Hutchinson

As the 100th FA Cup Final to be played, the 1981 final was always going to be the centre of much media attention. However, the presence of two members of Argentina's World Cup winning squad of 1978, who had joined Spurs that same summer, guaranteed intense interest beyond Britain's shores; on the eve of the final there was a television link up between Ossie Ardiles and Ricky Villa, the two Argentineans in question, and their respective families back in Buenos Aires. There was also the success of the Spurs' squad's Cup final song, *Ossie's Dream (Spurs Are On Their Way To Wembley)*, further adding to the weight of expectation on both sides, and Spurs and their Argentinean duo in particular.

The first meeting between the two sides was almost as predicted; City were determined and forceful, with their game plan seemingly to knock Spurs off their stride at every opportunity. For their part Spurs had expected that their greater craft in midfield, especially from Ardiles and Glenn Hoddle, would open City up in defence, allowing the twin strike force of Steve Archibald and Garth Crooks to plunder Spurs to victory in their sixth FA Cup Final. City's more battling qualities held sway, however, with Tommy Hutchinson producing a diving header in the 29th minute to give them the lead.

Whilst Ardiles struggled to impose himself, Ricky Villa was totally anonymous and after 68 minutes manager Keith Burkinshaw brought on the youthful and more direct Gary Brooks. Disappointment at being substituted or annoyance at his performance prompted Villa to walk around the Wembley pitch rather than take a seat alongside the manager, but somewhere along the long and lonely walk he realised the folly of his actions and made his way to the Spurs bench. He arrived just in time to see a Glenn Hoddle free-kick being deflected past Joe Corrigan in the City goal by Hutchinson, who thus joined a small band of players who had scored in FA Cup finals for both sides. Extra time brought more stalemate, prompting the first Wembley replay in history.

Villa's original perceived snub of his manager had not impressed his team-mates, who believed he should be dropped from the side for the replay the following Thursday. Burkinshaw however

selected exactly the same line-up for the match, ensuring Villa had an opportunity to make amends. It took him just seven minutes to erase the disappointment of five days previously, for an Ardiles shot rebounded to Archibald, whose own shot was saved by Corrigan but fell invitingly to Villa, loitering some seven yards from the City goal. He fired home the opening goal and set off on a meandering run towards the halfway line in celebration, a taster for what was to come later.

Whilst City played with just as much vigour and endeavour as previously, Spurs managed to match them in the key areas of the field, making the game a much more open and exciting spectacle than the first meeting. City equalised three minutes after Spurs took the lead, Steve MacKenzie volleying home from 20 yards after Hutchinson had laid the ball square. It was, agreed most pundits, one of the finest goals to grace a Wembley final and one which would be hard to top. The pundits and crowd didn't have too long to wait.

With the play flowing from end to end, both defences were put under considerable pressure. Four minutes into the second half Spurs' defence buckled, Paul Miller and Chris Hughton failing to deal with a long ball and allowing speedy winger Dave Bennett to find space between them before being manhandled to the ground. Despite fierce Spurs protests, Keith Hackett awarded a penalty and Kevin Reeves put the ball beyond Milija Aleksic to put City ahead.

Spurs had panicked when behind on Saturday; this time they showed patience, confident the goals they needed would come. On 70 minutes they drew level again, Glenn Hoddle collecting the ball on the edge of the penalty area from a corner and, eschewing the instinct to blast it goalwards, sent a high lob into the area. It fell to the feet of Archibald, whose first touch seemed to put the ball closer to Corrigan than the Spurs striker, but before either could pounce, Garth Crooks appeared to fire home the equaliser.

Six minutes later, just as the match was entering its final 15 minutes, came the winning goal. There appeared no danger whatsoever when Tony Galvin played the ball to Ricky Villa, well away from City's goal. But Villa picked up a bit of pace, drawing and beating Tommy Caton, Ray Ranson and the recovered Caton a second time before switching inside. Now there was panic in the City area, for Nicky Reid was also unable to get anywhere near the Spurs player, prompting Corrigan to rush from his goal. Just as Corrigan arrived at the six-yard line, and with Caton having recovered once again, Villa slipped the ball under the keeper for a magical, inventive and unbelievable winner. His victory run was just as special, evading as many Spurs players as he had City ones! Thus, the 100th FA Cup Final had delivered the match it promised and a goal worthy of winning the cup.

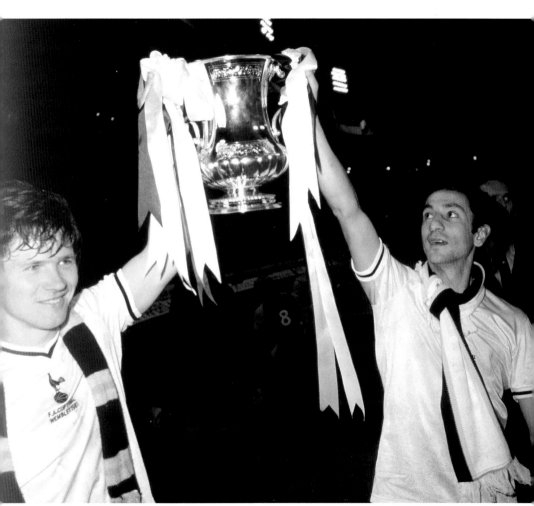

ITALY v
BRAZIL 3-2

World Cup Quarter-final – Barcelona 5/7/1982

Italy:
Zoff, Collovati (Bergomi), Gentile, Scirea, Cabrini, Oriali, Antognoni, Tardelli, (Marini), Conti, Graziani, Rossi

Brazil:
Valdir Peres, Leandro, Oscar, Luizinho, Junior, Cerezo, Falcao, Socrates, Zico, Serginho (Paulo Isidoro), Eder

There has hardly been a World Cup where Brazil wasn't firmly established as pre-tournament favourites. Their performance in winning three out of four tournaments between 1958 and 1970 (only England in 1966 saw them fall short) was largely responsible for the perennial confidence, but the country's ability to constantly unearth supremely talented players meant they were always likely to be there or thereabouts.

The 1982 competition held in Spain was no different. There were many pundits who believed Brazil possessed an even better side this time around than the 1970 winning side. Whilst 1970 had seen Pelé at his peak, aided and abetted by the likes of Jairzinho, Rivelino and Tostao, the 1982 vintage boasted two of the finest midfield players of their generation in Socrates and Zico. This was the creative hub of the side, also able to weigh in with vital goals, as they proved in an unblemished first group stage, winning all three matches with 10 goals scored and only two conceded.

By comparison, their Italian opponents were believed to be little more than a side in transition. Whilst they had discarded much of the catenaccio defence, they still lacked any real creative edge, preferring on many occasions to soak up pressure and hit teams on the break. Their first-round experience had seen them fail to win a single match, drawing all three, and only advancing into the next stage courtesy of having scored more goals than Cameroon. Coach Enzo Bearzot had tried to instil a club feeling about his squad, even going so far as selecting almost half the Juventus side. This included Paolo Rossi, an acknowledged goalscorer who had spent the previous two years on the sidelines after getting caught up in a gambling scandal – initially banned for three years, it was reduced to two on appeal and he only came back into the game just in time for the World Cup, with his selection being seen as controversial to say the least.

Rossi was completely anonymous in the group matches, with some reporters describing him as little better than a ghost wandering aimlessly around the pitch. He wasn't much better in the opening second-round group match, in the so-called Group of Death against Argentina, but fortunately Cabrini and Tardelli were alert enough to score the goals that enabled Italy to win 2-1

and put holders Argentina on the brink of elimination. A couple of days later Brazil finished off the job, winning 3-1 with a performance that screamed 'potential World Champions'.

The 3-1 victory did something else too, for it seemingly gave Brazil an additional advantage going into the make or break match with Italy – the extra goal scored meant Brazil needed only a draw to advance into the semi-finals; Italy had to win.

The only problem was that Brazil are never at their best when they only require a draw. It undoubtedly played on the minds of the Brazilian side, unsure whether to try and press forward to ensure victory or sit back and settle for what they had. Italy were waiting to pounce, not once, as previous Italian sides had done, but a total of three times.

It was an intense and pulsating match, with the action flowing from one end to the other. The first goal took just five minutes to arrive, Cabrini setting up an unmarked Rossi to give Italy the lead. It took Brazil just seven minutes to draw level, Zico turning past Claudio Gentile before slotting the ball through for Socrates who coolly placed it past Dino Zoff.

On 25 minutes the Brazilian defence made its second mistake of the day, Toninho Cerezo gifting the ball to Rossi who nipped away to restore Italy's lead. Whilst Rossi was already assured of the headlines the following day, several of his team-mates raised their own games to ensure Italy remained ahead, not least veteran goalkeeper Dino Zoff. Although aged 40 at the time of the 1982 competition, Zoff had been a member of the squad since 1970 and used all of his experience to keep out a barrage of Brazilian shots. He was finally beaten on 68 minutes, Falcao scoring the equaliser that at that stage gave Brazil the advantage in qualification.

Undeterred, Italy swept back into the attack. On 74 minutes their pressing led to a corner that was only partially cleared and Marco Tardelli fired in towards the danger area. Both Paolo Rossi and Francesco Graziani instinctively swung at the ball, Rossi made a meaningful connection and Italy were ahead for a third time, again the beneficiaries from some slack Brazilian defending.

With time running out to save their challenge, Brazil became ever more desperate. Socrates had the ball in the net only for the effort to be disallowed, but so did Antognoni for Italy. Dino Zoff pulled off another world class save in the final moments to further deny the South Americans and eventually time was up, Italy were through and Brazil went out. It was generally agreed that had Brazil a defence and strike force to match their undoubted midfield superiority, they would have won, but football is seldom won by agreement. Besides, Paolo Rossi had just hit a rich vein of form, one that was to see him score both Italy's goals in their 2-0 win over Poland in the semi-final and one of the goals by which Italy won the World Cup 3-1 against West Germany.

AS ROMA v LIVERPOOL 1-1

European Cup Final – Rome, 30/5/1984

Liverpool:
Grobbelaar, Neal, Lawrenson, Hansen, A Kennedy, Lee, Johnston (Nicol), Whelan, Souness, Rush, Dalglish (Robinson)

AS Roma:
Tancredi, Nappi, Bonetti, Righetti, Nela, Conti, Di Bartolomei, Cerezo (Strukelj), Falcao, Pruzzo (Chierico), Graziani

England were the dominant force in European Cup football at the end of the 1970s and early 1980s, winning the competition six years in succession thanks to Liverpool (with three victories), Nottingham Forest (two) and Aston Villa between 1977 and 1982. The run was ended with Hamburg's victory over Juventus in 1983, with both England's entrants, Aston Villa (as holders) and Liverpool (League champions) slipping out relatively early in the competition.

Liverpool qualified again for the 1983-84 competition but with a significantly different side to that which had triumphed in 1981. The key change had been in goal, where the dependable and safe Ray Clemence had been replaced by the extrovert and eccentric Bruce Grobbelaar. They say goalkeepers have to be mad, but no one was quite as mad as Grobbelaar. Yet, whilst he would celebrate winning a major game by walking on his hands, he was often to be found making a key save here, a telling interception there and ensuring Liverpool were in with the chance of winning further silverware.

Liverpool's path to the 1984 final had seen off OB Odense, Bilbao (by a single goal over two legs), Benfica (managed by Sven Goran Eriksson) and Dinamo Bucharest, winning the semi-final against the latter club with home and away victories for a 3-1 aggregate victory. Their opponents were to be the Italian champions Roma, whose own path had included overcoming a 2-0 first leg semi-final deficit against Dundee United with a 3-0 win in front of their vociferous fans. The good news for Roma was that the final was being held at the Olympico Stadium in Rome, their own stadium, in front of those same vociferous fans!

Although greatly outnumbered on the night, the thousands of Liverpool fans who journeyed to Rome did a more than passable job of recreating the Kop atmosphere within their section of the ground. They were boosted by the fact that all of their major players were free from injury and in the side, including Graeme Souness, Kenny Dalglish and Ian Rush, all of whom had played key roles in getting Liverpool to the final in the first place.

Roma were not without their own stars, not least Brazilian Falcao, but on the night the Liverpool midfield out-muscled the slender Brazilian, who was on the periphery of the match all night. He was not alone in the Roma side,

for Pruzzo was struggling with a stomach complaint and contributed little, and Graziani found that age had caught up with him just before Liverpool's defenders did.

Against the odds, for there was still a hostile and partisan crowd to deal with, Liverpool started the brighter and worked hard to try and silence the crowd. After 16 minutes Liverpool mounted the first serious challenge of the night and Phil Neal, who had scored in Liverpool's first European Cup triumph in 1977, repeated the trick with the opening goal. At last Roma were stirred into action and dominated for the next 20 minutes or so. Liverpool weathered the initial storm but eventually succumbed, Pruzzo backheeling the ball into the net for about his only meaningful contribution.

The goal served to inspire Roma after the break, but Liverpool again held firm and had their own period of domination as the game headed towards the final whistle. The final 15 minutes of normal time belonged to Liverpool but they could find no further way through a packed Roma defence, sending the game into extra time.

The only chances to be found in the additional half an hour were half chances, all spurned, so for the second time that season, a major European trophy would be decided by a penalty shoot out (Spurs had already won the UEFA Cup in similar fashion).

The first major surprise was the list of nominated penalty takers from Roma; Falcao had contributed little or nothing during the 120 minutes of action and decided the penalties weren't for him either, a snub from which his career at Roma never recovered (he made just four further appearances in the club's colours). Steve Nichol stepped up for Liverpool to set the shoot out in motion and sent the ball sailing high into the Rome night sky. Fortunately for him, Conti did much the same for Roma's second penalty, thus ensuring the two sides were level. Liverpool then scored their next three to keep the pressure firmly on Roma, who were suffering from all kinds of nerves, not least the fact that as the home side they were expected to win.

Their cause was not helped by the antics of Bruce Grobbelaar. As each Italian stepped up to take their kick, the Liverpool goalkeeper would wobble his legs, as if trying to indicate that he too was suffering from first night nerves. He was suffering from nothing of the sort, of course, but it served to separate the men from the boys on the Roma side. Thus Francesco Graziani came to the plate to take Roma's fourth kick with his side 3-2 behind – whether he caught sight of Grobbelaar or not isn't known, but his kick went the way of Nichol's and Conti's before him. Alan Kennedy, who'd scored the only goal of the game in the 1981 final against Real Madrid then strode up knowing that if he scored Liverpool couldn't be caught – he fired home past Franco Tancredi to win Liverpool their fourth European Cup.

ARGENTINA v ENGLAND 2-1

World Cup Quarter-final – Mexico City 22/6/1986

Argentina:
Pumpido, Ruggeri, Cuviuffo, Olarticoechea, Brown, Giusti, Batista, Burruchaga (Tapia), Enrique, Maradona, Valdano

England:
Shilton, Stevens, Sansom, Hoddle, Butcher, Fenwick, Steven (Barnes), Reid (Waddle), Lineker, Beardsley, Hodge

Ever since the notorious clash in the World Cup quarter-final of 1966, there had been a deep dislike between England and Argentina. Manager Alf Ramsey's 'animals' comments had not gone down well with the South Americans, who believed their eventual defeat was due to a European conspiracy against South American teams during that tournament. It was to be eight years before the two teams met again in a friendly at Wembley after Ramsey had departed the England job, with honours being shared in a 2-2 draw.

Two further friendlies had been staged, in Buenos Aires and at Wembley again, and both had passed without incident. But then, in 1982, the two countries were involved in an altogether different kind of clash, the Argentine invasion of the Falkland Islands prompting a British response in the form of a Task Force that journeyed 8,000 miles to retake the islands by force. There had been fears that the countries would meet at some stage during the 1982 World Cup, although Scotland were more likely to have met Argentina first. In the event all three countries were eliminated before they had a chance to lock horns.

Although the Falklands War was four years in the past, it added a distinct flavour to the footballing meeting between England and Argentina in the 1986 quarter-final. Largely forgotten were the two sides' pedigree in reaching that stage; Argentina had won three and drawn the other of their four matches thus far and had topped their group ahead of world champions Italy. England meanwhile had stuttered through the early stages, only confirming their qualification for the knockout stage with a 3-0 victory over Portugal before stepping up a gear in the second round against Paraguay.

Argentina relied heavily on Maradona, who had exorcised the ghosts of his experiences four years earlier (he had been sent off against Brazil) to produce some exciting performances. Up against him in midfield would be Glenn Hoddle, restored to the England side after the enforced

absence of Bryan Robson (a long term injury) and Ray Wilkins (suspended). That the match was potentially one of the key games of the tournament resulted in a crowd of 114,580 packing into the national stadium in Mexico City.

The first half passed without incident, sporting or diplomatic, although there was reportedly a hostile atmosphere on the terraces, where gangs of Argentinean supporters roamed looking for any Englishmen they could find; fortunately there were no major outbreaks of trouble.

The match exploded into life five minutes into the second half and resulted in a goal that is still hotly debated on either side of the Atlantic. An attempted clearance by Steve Hodge failed to make any distance away from the England goal, instead ballooning high up into the air in the England penalty area. It appeared to be falling down about eight yards from the England goalline, prompting England keeper Peter Shilton to come off his line to deal with the perceived threat. At the same time Diego Maradona moved in to contest the ball. Whilst Peter Shilton, at six foot, enjoyed a considerable height advantage over his opponent, he did not jump that high, attempting to punch the ball clear. Maradona had jumped higher than Shilton, but he'd also raised his fist too and in an instant had punched the ball into the empty England net. Maradona wheeled away in celebration, Shilton and numerous others indicated to the referee that a handball had occurred. Neither the referee nor his linesman appeared to have witnessed the incident, or if they had, believed Maradona to have headed the ball home, and so indicated that the goal would stand. Referee Ali Ben Naceur was surrounded by astonished and angry Englishmen but refused to change his decision – England were a goal down.

Five minutes later Maradona extended Argentina's lead, this time legitimately, with a goal of sublime quality. He collected the ball 10 yards inside his own half and spun away from the first England player to pose a threat. Off he went on a run, evading tackle after tackle, lunge after lunge, until finally he was in the penalty area once again. Shilton raced from his line but was beaten by another Maradona dummy to leave the Argentinean with an empty goal, stroking the ball home from a tight angle.

Falling two goals behind demanded a desperate England response and manager Bobby Robson sent on two wingers, Chris Waddle and John Barnes, with instructions to run at the Argentine defence. Barnes did just that, pulling the ball back from near the goalline to find Gary Lineker at the far post and with a simple tap in to bring England back into the game. A few minutes later Barnes and Lineker nearly reproduced the goods, but this time Lineker's lunge at the ball was inches away from connecting and the ball sailed harmlessly wide of the goal. That was to prove the last meaningful chance England created and Argentina advanced into the semi-finals.

Not surprisingly, the post-match interviews centred not on the superb solo goal Maradona had scored but his punch that had given Argentina the lead. Attempting to justify his actions by referencing the Malvinas, Maradona claimed the goal had been scored by the 'hand of God', a turn of phrase that was even more repugnant than the manner of the goal. With Argentina winning the next World Cup meeting between the two sides in 1998, it was to take 16 years before England got a measure of revenge, thanks to a 1-0 victory in 2002.

LIVERPOOL v EVERTON 3-2

FA Cup Final – Wembley 20/5/1989

Liverpool:
Grobbelaar, Ablett, Staunton (Venison), Nicol, Whelan, Hansen, Beardsley, Aldridge (Rush), Houghton, Barnes, McMahon

Everton:
Southall, McDonald, Van Den Hauwe, Ratcliffe, Watson, Bracewell (McCall), Nevin, Steven, Sharp, Cottee, Sheedy (Wilson)

Liverpool had reached the FA Cup final in 1988, where they had been surprisingly beaten by Wimbledon at Wembley. In the semi-final they had overcome the stern challenge of Brian Clough's Nottingham Forest at Hillsborough, and 12 months later the two sides were drawn against each other at the same penultimate stage, with Hillsborough again selected as the venue.

The game itself was just three minutes old and Peter Beardsley had just hit the bar when disaster struck. In order to alleviate the crush outside the stadium at the Leppings Lane end, a gate was opened and hundreds of fans swarmed onto the already packed terraces. A total of 95 were to die that afternoon, with a further fan dying some time later, the worst disaster to have hit British football. After days of mourning and argument, it was decided to continue the FA Cup as a tribute to those who had lost their lives, with Liverpool beating Forest in the replayed semi-final at Old Trafford to join city rivals Everton, who had seen off the challenge of Norwich City in their semi-final.

It was fitting that Liverpool should face Everton in the final, for there were countless families in Liverpool that had mixed allegiance to the two major sides of the city – they could share their grief and show the face of togetherness at the Wembley final.

In many respects the result was unimportant as the game in general struggled to come to terms with the enormity of what had happened. That Liverpool and Everton conspired to produce a game of high quality and drama did much to lift the spirits of the nation.

The match took just four minutes to explode into life, Footballer of the Year Steve Nicol setting Steve McMahon free on the right wing to bear down on the Everton goal. Whilst most of the defence were expecting a high ball aimed towards John Aldridge, McMahon sent in a low cross just in front of the Liverpool striker. Able to hit the ball first time without the need to readjust his feet, Aldridge swept the ball high into the Everton net for the opening goal.

Liverpool dominated the game thereafter but were unable to add to their winning margin. For their part Everton battled bravely, but their attacks were too few and too limited in their execution

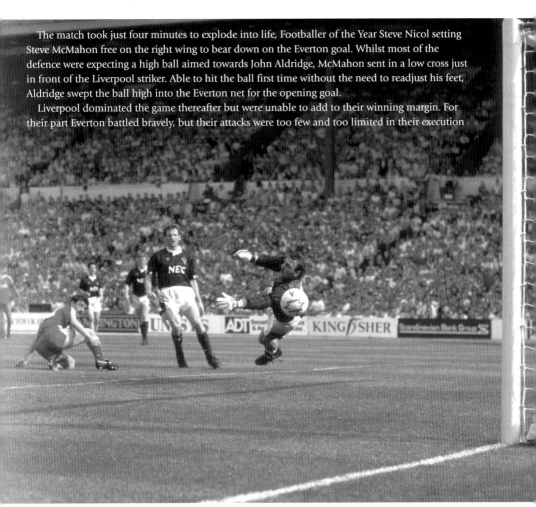

and the midfield was being almost totally overrun. Everton then took off the largely ineffectual Paul Bracewell and put on Stuart McCall, a battling all-action runner who initially served to inspire his team-mates into action.

For a short spell Everton held the upper hand even though they were unable to find a way through to goal. Liverpool manager Kenny Dalglish made his own change, taking off the exhausted scorer John Aldridge and replacing him with the master predator Ian Rush. Everton's final change came with the introduction of Ian Wilson for Kevin Sheedy and at last the Toffeemen showed a sense of urgency and upped the pace.

The match had entered its final minute and many on the Liverpool bench were checking their watches when Everton launched a final, desperate challenge on goal. Dave Watson found himself with space on the right and sent in what appeared to be a shot, although it was unlikely to enter the goal. Bruce Grobbelaar parried the ball away, only to see it land at the feet of the lurking Stuart McCall who swept home an unlikely equaliser. There was barely time for the match to restart before the referee blew to indicate extra time would be required.

Although crestfallen at having being caught so late, Liverpool started extra time the livelier. Six minutes into the first period they restored their lead, Nicol finding Rush inside the penalty area, although Rush had his back to goal and was closely marked by Kevin Ratcliffe. After feinting one way and turning the other, Rush took aim and fired high past Southall into the net.

Everton refused to be beaten however, and six minutes later McCall scored his second of the match (thus becoming the first substitute to score twice in an FA Cup final), collecting the ball on his chest and volleying home from 20 yards. Undeterred Liverpool pressed on and three minutes later got their noses in front again, Ian Rush equalling McCall's record of three minutes earlier and becoming the second substitute to score twice in an FA Cup final with a header from a John Barnes cross.

This time there was to be no coming back for Everton and Liverpool held on to win the trophy, probably the most apt of winners in light of the Hillsborough disaster of a month earlier. Unfortunately, although the Wembley authorities had removed the perimeter fencing at the stadium for the final, there were a number of mini pitch invasions throughout the match. Whilst many of these were good natured, the fact there were any at all was not in keeping with the solemnity of the day. That Liverpool's own lap of honour had to be abandoned was disappointing and hardly in the memory of those who died at Hillsborough. Liverpool meanwhile had other thoughts on their mind; they were still on track to record another double, with just one League match left to play.

ROYAL
LIVER
ASSURANCE

LIVERPOOL v
ARSENAL 0-2

League Match – Anfield 26/5/1989

Liverpool:
Grobbelaar, Ablett, Staunton, Nicol, Whelan, Burrows, Houghton, Aldridge, Rush (Beardsley), Barnes, McMahon

Arsenal:
Lukic, Dixon, Winterburn, Thomas, O'Leary, Adams, Rocastle, Richardson, Smith, Bould (Hayes), Merson (Groves)

Not since 1952 had the top two sides in the League met in the final League match of the season to decide which one would win the title. That previous occasion had seen Arsenal face Manchester United at Old Trafford needing to win by seven goals in order to win the title – they lost 6-1, a defeat of such severity they were pipped for second place too!

The 1989 clash between Liverpool and Arsenal at Anfield was an altogether different type of occasion. Originally scheduled for earlier in the season, the match had been postponed owing to the Hillsborough disaster and, with Liverpool's continued involvement in the FA Cup, re-scheduled for the Thursday following the final, which Liverpool duly won with a 3-2 victory over Everton. Thus Liverpool stood on the brink of winning the double for the second time in three years and becoming the first side to have won two doubles.

For much of the season it appeared as though the title was there for Arsenal to take. Last crowned champions in 1971, Arsenal had headed the table since December, moving to the top with a 3-2 victory over Charlton. Their slips following their ascendency had been few and far between, but in sight of the finishing post they lost at home to Derby County 2-1 and then could only draw with Wimbledon to hand the initiative back to the Anfield club. Going into the final match, Liverpool had 76 points and a goal record of having scored 65 and conceded 26 for a difference of +39 whilst Arsenal were on 73 points having scored 71 goals and conceded 36 for a difference of +35. For Arsenal to take the title, they would have to win by two or more goals in order to triumph by virtue of having scored more goals. Liverpool were in the midst of a 24-match unbeaten run, whilst Arsenal had lost their previous seven visits to Anfield, and the last time Liverpool had lost by two goals at home was more than four years previously – the omens did not look good for the London club.

Arsenal took to the field bearing bouquets to distribute to the four corners of the ground in recognition of the Hillsborough disaster. It was a gesture much appreciated by the Liverpool crowd even if they weren't exactly going to warm to the visitors! Perhaps it was the energy expended the previous Saturday in the Cup final, but for some reason the Anfield crowd was in a subdued mood. Whilst Arsenal continued taking the game to their hosts, that mood was unlikely to change, turning on its head any home advantage Liverpool might have expected.

For all their territorial advantage, however, Arsenal were unable to find the goals they needed. Liverpool were content to sit back and soak up the pressure, a tactic out of character for a side that had plenty of flair players in forward positions, but starved of any meaningful service, Aldridge and Rush contributed little.

The game was still goalless going into the second half, but soon after the restart Arsenal were awarded a free-kick deep in the Liverpool half. The referee indicated an indirect kick, which Nigel Winterburn sent sailing into the area. Alan Smith rose and and got the merest of flicks onto the ball, which went past the agonised dive of Grobbelaar and into the net for the opening goal. There were heated arguments by the Liverpool players that Smith had not touched the ball and that Winterburn's free-kick had gone directly into the goal, but the linesman confirmed Smith's touch to verify the goal. Smith's goal served to further inspire Arsenal and send Liverpool even further back into defence, Arsenal hoping to score before time ran out and Liverpool doing all they could to prevent it.

Time was almost up when John Lukic threw the ball out of his area, being worked quickly up the right wing for one last throw of the dice. A cross was flicked on by Alan Smith and fell invitingly to the feet of the advancing Michael Thomas. As he evaded Steve Nicol's desperate challenge, the goal appeared to be opening up in front of him, with television commentator Brian Moore commenting 'it's all up for grabs now' just as Thomas slipped the ball past Grobbelaar for an unexpected winner.

The whistle blew almost immediately after to signal it was Arsenal's title. Had Liverpool played with the same kind of panache they had during the course of the season, they would undoubtedly have won. Instead they sat back, almost inviting Arsenal to try and get the two goals they required. They had come up against a determined Arsenal side, as Michael Thomas later confirmed. 'The anticipation of it all. That's what stands out for me. Everyone had written us off and we just wanted to get out there and do the business.' No one did the business as well as Michael Thomas that evening. After helping Arsenal to a second title two years later, he moved on to join Liverpool, helping them win the FA Cup at the end of his first season.

ENGLAND v WEST GERMANY 1-1

World Cup Semi-final – Turin 4/7/1990

England:
Shilton, Pearce, Walker, Butcher (Steven), Parker, Wright, Waddle, Gascoigne, Beardsley, Lineker, Platt

West Germany:
Illgner, Brehme, Kohler, Augenthaler, Berthold, Buchwald, Hässler (Reuter), Matthäus, Thon, Völler (Riedle), Klinsmann

Ever since their extra-time defeat in the World Cup final of 1966, West Germany had had the advantage over England, winning the World Cup quarter-final in Mexico in 1970 (3-2 after extra time), the European Championship quarter-finals over two legs in 1972 (3-1 on aggregate) and the World Cup second group stage in 1982 (0-0, which eventually gave the Germans qualification for the semi-finals). There had even been two friendly victories over England since that 1982 World Cup match, 2-1 at Wembley the same year and 3-1 in Düsseldorf in 1987.

England's progress to the World Cup semi-finals in 1990, the furthest they had gone since that 1966 victory, had been chequered. Unconvincing in the group matches, they had only assured their progress by beating Egypt in the final match after draws against the Republic of Ireland and Holland. Their win against Belgium in the second round had come in the very last minute of extra time, whilst in the quarter-final they had had to come from behind before beating Cameroon thanks to two penalties by Gary Lineker. Just as four years previously, injury to Bryan Robson had prompted a rethink in team selection, with England looking stronger when Paul Gascoigne started orchestrating the side.

The Germans meanwhile had been in impressive form, topping their group and seeing off Holland in a volatile second round match before doing the same to Czechoslovakia in the second round. With host nation Italy having been eliminated the night before after a penalty shoot out against Argentina, West Germany had an opportunity of setting up a repeat of the 1986 final.

If the quality of football prior to the England and West Germany clash had been low, then this match changed all of that. England had much the better of the first half, with Paul Gascoigne forcing Illgner into a smart save with a low volley and the England defence restricting the German attack into several long range chances that did not trouble Peter Shilton. The opening goal,

however, had an element of farce to it. Stuart Pearce committed a foul on Thomas Hässler just outside the England penalty area on the hour mark. An England wall lined up to prevent a direct shot on goal, so Hässler laid the ball square to Andreas Brehme. He shot first time, only to see the ball strike the onrushing Paul Parker. The ball looped up high in the air and eventually fell just behind the despairing arms of Peter Shilton.

England avoided resorting to kick and rush, preferring to continue trying to forge out solid chances and, with 10 minutes left, finally succeeded in getting the ball to Gary Lineker inside the German penalty area. This time he managed to twist his way past a defender and in the same movement shot towards goal, the ball evading Illgner and hitting the back of the net for England's equaliser.

The final 10 minutes produced no further goals, meaning extra time, just as in 1970. Neither side managed any further goals, but the major incident of extra time was the booking picked up by Paul Gascoigne. Whilst he was always someone who played on the edge, he had managed to keep his enthusiasm in check during the match. Indeed, despite the fact that this was a World Cup semi-final, the game was played in excellent spirit throughout by both sides, further adding to the enjoyment of the watching millions. Nine minutes into extra time Gascoigne began a run that took him past two German players, but he appeared to have knocked the ball too far forward and into the path of Thomas Berthold. Gascoigne lunged at the ball, made contact with Berthold and was horrified to see the German collapse, supposedly in agony. Gascoigne's cause wasn't helped by the reaction of the German bench, who rose waving their arms around to indicate that they thought the challenge deserved a card. The Brazilian referee obviously agreed, for he brandished a yellow card at Gascoigne. It was his second of the tournament, meaning he would miss the final should England qualify. For a few moments the distraught player was lost in his own world, tears welling in his eyes until he was able to compose himself and get on with the job of trying to ensure his team-mates would get through.

Extra time produced no further goals, although both Chris Waddle and Guido Buchwald hit the post, so just as in the first semi-final, a penalty shoot out was required to try and separate the two sides. The first six were all scored, Lineker, Beardsley and Platt for England and Brehme, Matthäus and Riedle for West Germany. Then Stuart Pearce stepped up to take England's fourth kick, only to see the ball strike Illgner's legs. Thon scored his kick to give West Germany advantage for the first time, meaning Chris Waddle had to score to keep England in the competition. Instead his kick disappeared high into the Turin night, gifting West Germany a place in the final. They would eventually get their revenge over Argentina, winning 1-0 in a dreadful showcase final.

ENGLAND v HOLLAND 4-1

European Championship Match – Wembley 18/6/1996

England:
Seaman, G Neville, Pearce, Ince (Platt), Southgate, Adams, Anderton, Gascoigne, Shearer (Fowler), Sheringham (Barmby), McManaman

Holland:
Van Der Sar, Reiziger, Blind, Bogarde, Winter, Seedorf, Witschge (De Kock), De Boer (Kluivert), Cruijff, Bergkamp, Hoekstra (Cocu)

If Scotland as nearest neighbours and Germany (and its former entity West Germany) as perennial opponents had been the two sides England most liked to beat, then running them a close third was undoubtedly Holland. The two countries had met in four meaningful matches prior to their clash in the 1996 European Championships: a European Championship finals group match in 1988 in Germany, which the Dutch had won 3-1, a World Cup finals group match in Italy in 1990, which had finished goalless, and more recently two qualifying matches for the 1994 finals in the USA. Holland had recovered from being two goals down at Wembley to draw 2-2, whilst the return had seen the Dutch survive an England penalty scare, in which Ronald Koeman brought down David Platt and escaped with just a yellow card before going on to score Holland's first in a 2-0 win. The end result was England failed to qualify for the finals for the first time since 1978 and signalled the end of manager Graham Taylor's time in charge of the England side.

He was eventually replaced by Terry Venables, who was spared the trouble of qualifying for the next major tournament, the European Championships, which England were hosting. A hesitant draw against Switzerland followed by a 2-0 win over Scotland meant England had already qualified for the knockout stage by the time they came to face Holland, as had their opponents as long as they avoided a heavy defeat or Scotland failed to beat Switzerland in the other group match.

Whilst Holland had impressed during their World Cup campaign in the USA, they were something of an unknown quantity when they arrived in England. Internal disagreements, in particular between coach Gus Hiddink and Edgar Davids, which resulted in the player being sent home, had revealed the Dutch camp to be a disunited one, although they could still pose a threat to England's ambitions.

Instead, England produced one of their best performances in many a year. Alan Shearer gave them an early lead from the penalty spot after Paul Ince's run had been halted by Danny Blind. England pressed on throughout the first half although they were unable to add to their score before the break.

Five minutes into the second half, however, Paul Gascoigne floated over England's first corner of the half and found Teddy Sheringham on the penalty spot. A firm header towards goal was aided by Steve McManaman standing directly in front of Dutch keeper Edwin van der Sar, blocking his view of a ball he was convinced was going wide. McManaman moved out of the way in time for the ball to settle nicely in the bottom of the goal.

Sheringham then turned provider for Alan Shearer for England's third goal. Paul Gascoigne made a delightful run into the Dutch penalty area, muscling his way past his marker. A square ball then found Sheringham, whose feint to shoot drew two defenders to him to try and block, but instead Sheringham laid the ball off to the unmarked Shearer to fire home from 12 yards. It was a goal of real quality, one which the Dutch themselves might have trademarked during their 1970s heyday.

And England still weren't finished, pouring forward at every opportunity in search of further goals. Darren Anderton lined up a shot from just outside the area, only for the ball to strike Blind on his back. Although the deflection was minimal, it was enough to ensure Van Der Sar was unable to hold on to the ball, parrying it back into play. Whilst the keeper reacted quickly and was back on his feet in an instant, Teddy Sheringham was quicker, pouncing on the ball and steering it with precision past Van Der Sar's right hand and into the net. Whilst the goal was cheered with enthusiasm at Wembley, word of the goal sent Scottish fans at Villa Park into raptures, for with their side leading against Switzerland, England's four-goal advantage meant that the Dutch would be eliminated.

Holland rallied just enough to get the goal that gave them qualification from the group, substitute Patrick Kluivert slotting home after being put through by Dennis Bergkamp. In his short time on the field, Kluivert presented a considerable threat to England, which prompted questions as to why he had not been selected from the start.

The goal was enough to earn Holland qualification for the knock-out stage but the psychological damage had been done – they failed to score against France and went out after a penalty shoot out. England also failed to score in their quarter-final against Spain but managed to win their shoot out 4-2 to set up a clash with West Germany in the semi-final.

FRANCE v BRAZIL 3-0

World Cup Final – Paris 12/7/1998

France:
Barthez, Lizarazu, Desailly, Thuram, Leboeuf, Djorkkaeuff (Vieira), Deschamps, Zidane, Petit, Karembeu (Boghossian), Guivarc'h (Henry)

Brazil:
Taffarel, Cafu, Aldair, Junior Baiano, Roberto Carlos, Cesar Sampaio (Edmundo), Dunga, Rivaldo, Leonardo (Denilson), Ronaldo, Bebeto

The host nation is often installed as the favourite whenever the World Cup comes around, yet surprisingly few have actually gone on to win the competition – Uruguay in 1930, Italy in 1934, England in 1966, West Germany in 1974 and Argentina in 1978 were the only sides to have matched expectations.

France had first hosted the finals in 1938 but had gone out in the quarter-finals to holders and eventual champions Italy. Since then their World Cup pedigree left a lot to be desired, having got no further than the semi-finals, which they accomplished in 1958, 1982 and 1986. Their truly great side of the early 1980s, built around Michel Platini, might have achieved the feat, but for some cynical West German play in the 1982 semi-final. Instead, France had had to settle for becoming European champions only in 1984.

Fourteen years later another great French side had emerged, with an eccentric goalkeeper, a solid defence, one of the greatest midfield players of his era and an exceptional striking talent on the way to greatness. Fabien Barthez was the goalkeeper who put the excesses of his eccentricity behind him to help put France on the way to the final. The undoubted star of the French side was Zinedine Zidane, tall, strong and difficult to muscle off the ball and possessed with visionary skills that set up countless chances for his team-mates. He too held a dark side, one which emerged during a group match against Saudi Arabia and saw him stamp on an opponent, earning him a two-match ban. He returned to keep his temper in check and guide France into the final.

Their opponents Brazil were the holders, having won the competition four years previously thanks to a penalty shoot out against Italy. Their side in 1998 was effectively built around the striking talents of Rivaldo, Bebeto and especially, Ronaldo. All three in general but Ronaldo in

particular had been in good form on the run up to the final, but on the eve of the biggest game of his career, something of a disaster began to emerge. At some point during the evening, Ronaldo began complaining of feeling unwell, with some sources claiming he suffered a fit. He was rushed off to hospital for a series of tests, but in advance of the results, Brazilian coach Mario Zagalo decided that he was in no fit state to participate in a World Cup final and dropped him from the team. The decision sparked frantic behind-the-scenes activity, with Ronaldo later being reinstated into the side, with some claiming that it had been sponsors Nike who had exerted the pressure that forced Zagalo to reverse his selection.

Ronaldo did make it into the line-up for the start of the final and lasted the full 90 minutes, but his contribution to the action was limited to shaking hands with the French players prior to the start and again after they had won. At any level of the game it is difficult for 10 men to play against 11; Ronaldo's presence in the Brazilian side gave them a mountain to climb.

Brazil's task would have been difficult with a fully fit Ronaldo, for this was not a particularly great Brazilian side, easily nullified by a French side that raised their game on the day. It took the French only 27 minutes to put themselves in the lead, Zidane rising ahead of his defender at the near post to head home the opening goal. Just before half-time he repeated the dose, this time at the far post to give France an unassailable lead.

Mario Zagalo could have given Brazil a chance of getting back into the game by making changes at half-time. Ronaldo would have been the obvious choice, given that he had contributed nothing in the opening half, but perhaps Zagalo felt Ronaldo was capable of bursting into life at some point. Perhaps he was instructed to keep Ronaldo on the field by the sponsors!

Instead, he took Leonardo off a minute into the second half, replacing him with Denilson. The Brazilians got something of a boost on 68 minutes with Marcel Desailly collecting his second yellow card of the match and being sent off, but still proved unable to take advantage. Cesar Sampaio made way for Edmundo for the final 15 minutes but still could make no headway, and in the final minute Emmanuel Petit gave the scoreline a truer reflection of French superiority with a breakaway goal, the 1000th France had scored in the World Cup.

Whilst the action had been particularly one sided, with only the captain Dunga emerging from the game with any credit for his performance, the off the field controversy surrounding Ronaldo had overshadowed a fine French performance. Whilst the most ill-disciplined side of the tournament, with three players sent off, they were worthy winners of the final, with Zidane in particular redeeming his earlier tarnished reputation.

MANCHESTER UNITED v BAYERN MUNICH 2-1

European Cup Final – Barcelona, 26/5/1999

Manchester United:
Schmeichel, Neville, Johnsen, Stam, Irwin, Beckham, Butt, Giggs, Blomqvist (Sheringham), Yorke, Cole (Solskjær)

Bayern Munich:
Kahn, Matthäus (Fink), Babbel, Linke, Kuffour, Tarnat, Effenberg, Jeremies, Basler (Salihamidzic), Jancker, Zickler (Scholl)

When Manchester United won the European Champion Club's Cup in 1968, they were required to play nine matches, beating the national champions of Malta, Yugoslavia, Poland and Spain before overcoming Portuguese champions Benfica in the final. By the time they reached the final for a second time in 1999, they had played 12 matches just getting to the final, and not everyone they beat were their country's respective champions. Indeed, neither were United, having finished the 1997-98 season as runners-up to Arsenal, a point behind their London rivals.

It had been the major clubs desire for more money-spinning games that had prompted UEFA to change the format for the cup, which became the UEFA Champions League. It also averted any talk, at least at the time, of the major clubs forming their own breakaway European League. So Manchester United got an easy qualifying match to make the group stages and then just about qualified as one of the best runners-up, behind Bayern Munich.

United's form improved considerably after Christmas, topping the Premier League for much of the rest of the season and clinching the title with a 2-1 win over Spurs. The following week they won the FA Cup, their third double, but still in with a chance of lifting an unprecedented treble. Only Liverpool in 1977 had previously come close; they won the League and European Cup but lost in the final of the FA Cup, ironically against Manchester United.

United's opponents in the final were to be Bayern Munich, thus setting up another England and Germany clash. The two group matches between the sides had both finished draws, and both sides had enforced absences to contend with in the final, United being without their inspirational captain Roy Keane and Paul Scholes, whilst Bayern were missing top scorer Giovane Elber and full-back Bixente Lizarazu.

Without Keane's steadying influence, which had been an important factor in their success in the semi-final against Juventus, United looked nervy and unsure. Peter Schmeichel was making his last appearance for the club but it looked more like his first for the opening few minutes, his fluffed

clearances giving Bayern heart. The German side took the lead after just six minutes, Ronny Johnsen tripping Carsten Jancker and Mario Basler scoring from the resulting free-kick.

Despite falling a goal behind United seemed incapable of lifting their game, with both strikers Andy Cole and Dwight Yorke being largely ineffective and the midfield being overrun. Manager Alex Ferguson made his first change after 66 minutes, taking off Blomqvist and bringing on Teddy Sheringham. Whilst United pressed forward looking for an equaliser, ominous gaps began appearing at the back, which Bayern should have capitalised upon, hitting the post through Mehmet Scholl and the bar through Jancker.

Ferguson threw on Ole Gunnar Solskjær with 10 minutes left to play, but he fared little or no better in the remaining official time than his team-mates had in the preceding 80 minutes. The fourth official Fiorenzo Treossi held up the board to indicate there would be three minutes of added time, which seemed to be a signal for many of the disappointed United fans to start heading for the exits. Among them was George Best, one of their scorers when they had won the cup in 1968, who was out of the stadium and in a taxi heading back to his hotel when the drama began unfurling.

With time ticking down United pressed a corner. Goalkeeper Peter Schmeichel ran the full length of the field to lend his weight to the attack, having scored in a UEFA Cup match some years previously when United were similarly chasing the game. The corner never reached him, with Steffan Effenberg hooking the ball clear and seemingly away from danger. It fell to Ryan Giggs, who controlled the ball in an instant and let fly with a shot that looked to be heading wide of the goal. That was until Teddy Sheringham instinctively stuck out a leg and diverted it inside the right-hand post for an unlikely equaliser.

Everyone was convinced that the goal meant extra time. United put pressure on Bayern right from the restart, hoping to force the Germans back into their half of the field and use up whatever time still remained. That pressure led to Sami Kuffour conceding another corner, surely the last action of the game. This time Schmeichel decided against venturing up field, perhaps to conserve his energies for extra time. David Beckham's delivery this time arrived at the near post, where Sheringham was again lurking. His flick took the ball towards the far post, where the other substitute Ole Gunnar Solskjær was waiting to steer the ball into the roof of the net for United's second goal inside 90 seconds. Those United fans who had not left the stadium erupted in sheer delight, whilst the German players (and their fans) just could not believe what had happened. It had been a fairly mundane final for almost 90 minutes, but the final 90 seconds made it a truly memorable night for Manchester United and made a knight out of Alex Ferguson.

GERMANY v ENGLAND 1-5

World Cup Qualifier – Munich 1/9/2001

Germany:
Kahn, Rehmer, Worns (Asamoah), Nowotny, Linke, Boehme, Hamman, Deisler, Ballack (Klose), Jancker, Neuville (Kehl)

England:
Seaman, G Neville, Ferdinand, Campbell, Ashley Cole, Beckham, Gerrard (Hargreaves), Scholes (Carragher), Barmby (McManaman), Owen, Heskey

England had suffered a torrid European Championship finals tournament in 2000, finishing third in their group and missing out on progress into the knockout stage. The only piece of consolation, and it was small, was that they had beaten Germany and finished above them in the group. Many questioned the tactics employed by coach Kevin Keegan, who appeared unsure how to get the best out of the players at his disposal. With England being drawn in the same World Cup qualifying group as the Germans, there were considerable fears that England might have to settle for runners-up spot in the group and rely on the playoffs to book their place in the finals in Japan and South Korea.

Some of those fears came to be realised. England's opening match in qualification saw them play host to Germany at Wembley, the last match to be played at the stadium before it was to be dismantled and a new one built. Despite the pressure on England to achieve a good result, they played hesitatingly and lost 1-0. Immediately after the game Keegan announced his resignation, stating he had taken the team as far as he could. Caretaker Howard Wilkinson couldn't stop the rot either, England only drawing 0-0 away to Finland in his match in charge.

Keegan's eventual replacement was a major shock. In selecting Sven Goran Eriksson, the FA picked someone who was not English for the first time in their history. Eriksson was aware of the potential pitfalls, but if he could get England to the finals, all would be forgiven. Over the next few months England began picking up points in pursuit of Germany, but by the time they arrived in

Munich for the return fixture, they were still six points adrift and games were running out. The Germans had already posted a record of five wins and one draw in their six matches; victory over England would effectively seal top spot. To put England's task into an even bigger context, Germany had lost only one World Cup qualifier at home in their entire history!

After six minutes the job appeared to be done, Carsten Jancker giving the home side the lead after getting to a loose ball before David Seaman and prodding home the opening goal.

England did not let the strike unduly worry them, re-discovering their shape and drawing level seven minutes later. A partially cleared corner found Gary Neville some 40 yards from the German goal and his header back into the penalty area found many of the Germans rushing out to try and catch England offside. Nick Barmby, one of the smallest players on the England team, got to the ball before Oliver Kahn and nodded the ball down into the path of Michael Owen, who just got ahead of another German defender to knock the ball into an empty net.

Just before half-time England took the lead. David Beckham took a free-kick on the right flank, hitting a German defender and then sending the rebound into the area. Rio Ferdinand rose above everyone else and nodded the ball back for Steven Gerrard to unleash a 30-yard shot that skipped along the surface and hit the back of the net.

England continued using the same ploy of players nodding the ball down into danger areas in the second half and were rewarded three minutes after the restart with a third goal. This time it was Emile Heskey who got on the end of a Beckham cross and laid off a cushioned header for Michael Owen to perform a mid-air scissors kick and fire home to further extend England's lead.

By now England were running the Germans ragged and Owen completed his hat-trick after 66 minutes. Owen Hargreaves won the ball on the half-way line and spotted Michael Owen in space. A quickly slotted ball set Michael on his way and, waiting for Kahn to commit himself, coolly fired home from 15 yards just as he was about to be tackled.

Perhaps they sensed there was going to be no way back from such a deficit, but England's fourth goal was the signal for many of the German crowd to begin heading for the exits, even though there was more than 20 minutes left to play. They thus missed England's fifth, the much maligned Emile Heskey being put through by Paul Scholes, getting the ball seemingly stuck under his feet but recovering and striking home a fifth England goal past a hapless Oliver Kahn.

Whilst there were many who were prepared to put the result down as something of a freak (sides of the calibre of Germany don't usually lose 5-1 at home, even to sides of England's calibre), there was no doubting the style of England's play had continued to create chances, even when they had fallen behind. That they had a predator of Michael Owen's quality, ably supported by the long range shooting skills of Steven Gerrard and the vision of David Beckham, had produced both a result and a match that was truly memorable.

LIVERPOOL v
AC MILAN 3-3

European Cup Final – Istanbul 25/5/2005

Liverpool:
Dudek, Finnan (Hamann), Hyypia, Carragher, Traoré, Kewell (Smicer), Alonso, Gerrard, Riise, García, Baros (Cissé)

AC Milan:
Dida, Cafú, Stam, Nesta, Maldini, Seedorf (Serginho), Gattuso (Costa), Pirlo, Kaká, Crespo (Tomasson), Shevchenko

Liverpool had won the League championship 18 times and the European Cup four times by 2005, but their last success in the former had been in 1990 and the latter in 1984. Domestically they had been eclipsed by Manchester United and Arsenal, with both clubs adding to their tallies of League titles, even if only United had made progress in the European Cup. Even Chelsea, bankrolled by Roman Abramovich's billions, had overtaken Liverpool in the quest for honours.

Whilst Chelsea and their charismatic manager Jose Mourinho made most of the headlines during the 2004-05 season, Liverpool quietly got on with the job of making progress in both the Carling Cup and Champions League. They were to lose the final of the Carling Cup to Chelsea at Cardiff, but in defeat came knowledge, for Liverpool's own coach, Rafa Benitez was just as tactically astute as his Portuguese rival, he just didn't shout about it as much.

Thus when the two sides clashed in the semi-final of the Champions League, Benitez and Liverpool had a plan to counter Chelsea's threat. They were aided by the absence of Damien Duff and Arjen Robben, two players who normally played wide and gave Chelsea threat down the flanks. With neither available, Chelsea played much flatter and in the first leg at Stamford Bridge, Liverpool were able to nullify any threat to their own goal. Neither did they venture too far towards Chelsea's goal, but a goalless draw gave them every possibility of progress in the return leg. That ended up being settled by a hotly disputed Luis Garcia goal after four minutes; despite William Gallas hooking the ball back before it had crossed the line (so claimed Chelsea), the referee

awarded the goal and Liverpool were on their way to their sixth European Cup final and their first since the tragic events of Heysel 20 years previously.

Just as at Heysel they faced Italian opposition, this time in the form of AC Milan. Whereas the spectacle at Heysel had been blighted, this time the two protagonists put on a show worthy of the occasion, in front of a watching television audience of some three billion, in what was the fiftieth European Cup final.

With the prolific Andrei Shevchenko (soon to be bound for Chelsea) leading the line, ably supported by Herman Crespo (on loan from Chelsea) AC Milan were obviously going to be a threat up front and it took them just 53 seconds to fire themselves into the lead. Djimi Traore fouled Kaka and the resulting free-kick from the right wing was hooked home by the veteran skipper Paolo Maldini. If things had started badly for Liverpool they were to get significantly worse, for Harry Kewell had to limp from the field to be replaced by Vladimir Smicer, initially upsetting whatever rhythm Liverpool had managed. Then Shevchenko scored a second, only for his effort to be ruled out, wrongly as it later turned out, for offside. AC Milan didn't worry too much, creating two chances for Crespo to fire home to give AC Milan a supposedly unassailable three-goal lead going in at half-time.

What happened next depends on which camp you chose to believe. According to Liverpool, the AC Milan players came in at half-time convinced they had the cup won and celebrated during the 15-minute break loud enough for the noise to drift into the Liverpool dressing room. It certainly inspired Liverpool to increase their efforts after the break, looking for a goal at the very least with which to lift the spirits of their supporters. Benitez also made a tactical change, switching to three at the back and taking off another injured player in Steve Finnan and introducing the assured Hamann into the central midfield position.

In the space of six minutes, Liverpool not only got a goal to lift their supporters, they scored three to draw level. At the heart of all the action was captain Steve Gerrard, who started the revival with a header from John Arne Riise's cross after 53 minutes. Two minutes later the deficit was down to one goal as Smicer thumped the ball home off the goalkeeper's hands. Four minutes later the revival was complete, Gerrard being brought down in the penalty area and Xabi Alonso stabbing home a rebound after Dida had saved his initial effort.

The rest of the match settled into an intriguing battle, with neither side quite as penetrative as they had been in their earlier spells, meaning the game headed into extra time. There was to be only one clear cut chance, which fell to Shevchenko, who saw Jerzy Dudek save his first effort and then recover exceptionally well to block the rebound too. The general consensus at the time was that for either side to have lost, or won the game that late on would have been a travesty, with Dudek's double save enough to take the game into a penalty shoot out.

Jerzy Dudek had obviously done his homework, knowing which side the ball was likely to go and also employing the same kind of off-putting tactics last seen utilised by Bruce Grobbelaar 21 years previously. The key penalty came from Andrei Shevchenko; unable to score during the 120 minutes of action, he also saw his poorly hit penalty saved by Dudek, giving Liverpool their fifth European Cup. The fiftieth European Cup final had produced one of the most dramatic finishes of all, perfectly in keeping with the occasion.

ITALY v
FRANCE 1-1

World Cup Final – Berlin 9/7/2006

Italy:
Buffon, Zambrotta, Materazzi, Cannavaro, Grosso, Perrotta (Iaquinta), Pirlo, Gattuso, Camoranesi (Del Piero), Totti (De Rossi), Toni

France:
Barthez, Sagnol, Thuram, Gallas, Abidal, Vieira (Diarra), Makelele, Ribery (Trezeguet), Zidane, Malouda, Henry (Wiltord)

French defence of the World Cup won in some style in 1998 didn't last long, exiting the group stages in 2002 having failed to score and picking up only one point from a goalless draw. By the time qualification for the 2006 competition came around many of the triumphant side had retired, including Zidane, whilst others were quickly approaching the ends of their international careers.

With qualification looking increasingly unlikely owing to too many drawn games, Zidane was persuaded out of retirement and took an inspiring place in the side, guiding them to Germany with two points to spare. They made a slow start to the finals proper but began to pick up steam once the competition had reverted to a straight knockout competition, seeing off the fancied Spaniards, then Brazil and Portugal in the semi-finals to take their place in the final.

The other half of the draw had seen Italy emerge victorious, being fortunate to see off Australia before turning on the style against Croatia and then host nation Germany to reach their sixth final. For once, Italy were believed to have the brighter options up front, in contrast to their previous reliance on defence.

France survived an early scare when Thierry Henry clashed with Cannavaro early on and was left lying prostrate on the field. Although a stretcher appeared Henry duly picked himself up and carried on with the game. Henry was involved in the next piece of decisive action, heading on Fabien Barthez's long punt out of goal. The ball fell invitingly for Florent Malouda to burst into the Italian penalty area before being brought down by Materazzi's lunge after only seven minutes.

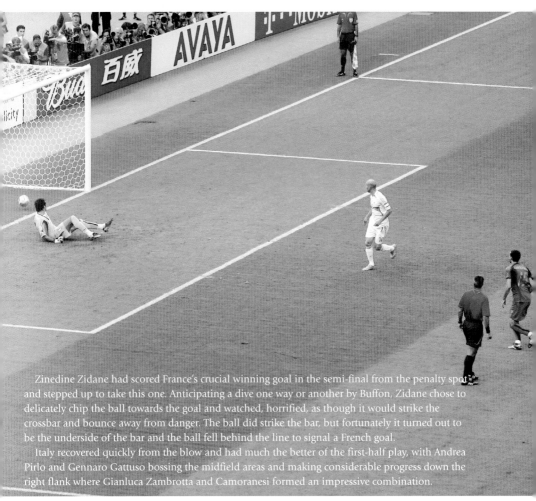

Zinedine Zidane had scored France's crucial winning goal in the semi-final from the penalty spot and stepped up to take this one. Anticipating a dive one way or another by Buffon, Zidane chose to delicately chip the ball towards the goal and watched, horrified, as though it would strike the crossbar and bounce away from danger. The ball did strike the bar, but fortunately it turned out to be the underside of the bar and the ball fell behind the line to signal a French goal.

Italy recovered quickly from the blow and had much the better of the first-half play, with Andrea Pirlo and Gennaro Gattuso bossing the midfield areas and making considerable progress down the right flank where Gianluca Zambrotta and Camoranesi formed an impressive combination.

Camoranesi's persistence earned Italy a corner after 19 minutes, which Pirlo sent sailing into the area. There was a suspicion that the ball had drifted out of play before arriving in the danger area, but Materazzi atoned for his earlier discretion by powering home an equalising header.

If Italy had been in control in the first half, then France returned the compliment in the second spell, with Thierry Henry in particular proving difficult to shake off the ball and linking up with Frank Ribery to cause the Italians considerable problems in defence. Despite this there were no further goals in normal time, prompting an extra 30 minutes of action.

Play switched from one end to the other during the 30 minutes, but it has tended to be completely overshadowed by a moment of madness from Zidane. A French attack had broken down and the ball was on its way towards the French half as Zidane and Materazzi made their way out of the Italian penalty area. Words were obviously exchanged between the pair, but what was said by Materazzi obviously touched a raw nerve with Zidane, for in an instant he had turned around, hurried up to his opponent and head-butted him in the chest.

Materazzi collapsed in a heap whilst other players stared in disbelief. The referee had obviously missed the incident and moved over to talk to the nearest assistant to see if he had spotted anything untoward. Judging by the television pictures he can't have seen anything either, but the fourth official, who had access to the television set, obviously did and pointed it out to Mr Elizondo. Zinedine Zidane, who had earlier joined an elite band of players who had scored in more than one World Cup final, thus joined an even more elite one; those who have been sent off in a final.

There was too little time remaining for Italy to make the one-man advantage count, which meant the game would be settled by a penalty shoot out, only the second World Cup final to be so decided. The first occasion, in 1994 in America, had seen Italy finish on the losing side after the normally reliable Franco Baresi and Roberto Baggio had missed their shots. Cool heads would be required to rectify that defeat.

History shows that all five Italians scored with their penalty kicks, with Grosso scoring the all important fifth. By then Italy were already ahead, David Trezeguet having hit the bar with his effort. Italy thus won their fourth world title, the circumstances surrounding it counting for little in their post match celebrations.

For Zidane, however, it meant an inglorious end to a glorious career. The highlight had been scoring with two headers in the 1998 World Cup final, the low spot undoubtedly different use of the head in the 2006 final.

ALSO AVAILABLE IN THIS SERIES

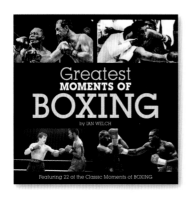

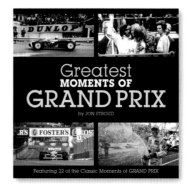

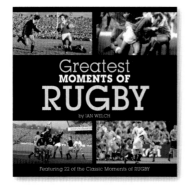

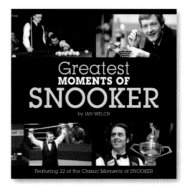

THE PICTURES IN THIS BOOK WERE PROVIDED COURTESY OF THE FOLLOWING:

GETTY IMAGES
101 Bayham Street, London NW1 0AG

PA PHOTOS
www.paphotos.com

Concept and Creative Direction:
VANESSA and KEVIN GARDNER

Design and Artwork: KEVIN GARDNER

Image research: ELLIE CHARLESTON

PUBLISHED BY GREEN UMBRELLA PUBLISHING

Publishers:
JULES GAMMOND and VANESSA GARDNER

Written by: GRAHAM BETTS